Activity Log Book

All rights reserved.

No part of this publication may be reproduced, distributed, or transmitted in any form or by any means, including photocopying, recording, or other electronic or mechanical methods, without the prior written permission of the publisher, except in the case of brief quotations embodied in critical reviews and certain other noncommercial uses permitted by copyright law. For permission requests, write to the publisher, **hdtenmediagroup@gmail.com** "Attn: Coordinator"

Ordering Information:
Special discounts are available on quantity purchases by corporations, associations, and others. For details, contact the publisher at **hdtenmediagroup@gmail.com**.

Cover Design by H. Daniel
Design Copyright © by HDTEN Media Group
All rights reserved.
ISBN: 10: 1721884327
ISBN: 13: 978-1721884322

Date	Time	Name	Phone Number	Subject	Follow-up Required	Initials	✓

Date	Time	Name	Phone Number	Subject	Follow-up Required	Initials	✓

Date	Time	Name	Phone Number	Subject	Follow-up Required	Initials	✓

Date	Time	Name	Phone Number	Subject	Follow-up Required	Initials	✓

Date	Time	Name	Phone Number	Subject	Follow-up Required	Initials	✓

Date	Time	Name	Phone Number	Subject	Follow-up Required	Initials	✓

Date	Time	Name	Phone Number	Subject	Follow-up Required	Initials	✓

Date	Time	Name	Phone Number	Subject	Follow-up Required	Initials	✓

Date	Time	Name	Phone Number	Subject	Follow-up Required	Initials	✓

Date	Time	Name	Phone Number	Subject	Follow-up Required	Initials	✓

Date	Time	Name	Phone Number	Subject	Follow-up Required	Initials	✓

Date	Time	Name	Phone Number	Subject	Follow-up Required	Initials	✓

Date	Time	Name	Phone Number	Subject	Follow-up Required	Initials	✓

Date	Time	Name	Phone Number	Subject	Follow-up Required	Initials	✓

Date	Time	Name	Phone Number	Subject	Follow-up Required	Initials	✓

Date	Time	Name	Phone Number	Subject	Follow-up Required	Initials	✓

Date	Time	Name	Phone Number	Subject	Follow-up Required	Initials	✓

Date	Time	Name	Phone Number	Subject	Follow-up Required	Initials	✓

Date	Time	Name	Phone Number	Subject	Follow-up Required	Initials	✓

Date	Time	Name	Phone Number	Subject	Follow-up Required	Initials	✓

Date	Time	Name	Phone Number	Subject	Follow-up Required	Initials	✓

Date	Time	Name	Phone Number	Subject	Follow-up Required	Initials	✓

Date	Time	Name	Phone Number	Subject	Follow-up Required	Initials	✓

Date	Time	Name	Phone Number	Subject	Follow-up Required	Initials	✓

Date	Time	Name	Phone Number	Subject	Follow-up Required	Initials	✓

Date	Time	Name	Phone Number	Subject	Follow-up Required	Initials	✓

Date	Time	Name	Phone Number	Subject	Follow-up Required	Initials	✓

Date	Time	Name	Phone Number	Subject	Follow-up Required	Initials	✓

Date	Time	Name	Phone Number	Subject	Follow-up Required	Initials	✓

Date	Time	Name	Phone Number	Subject	Follow-up Required	Initials	✓

Date	Time	Name	Phone Number	Subject	Follow-up Required	Initials	✓

Date	Time	Name	Phone Number	Subject	Follow-up Required	Initials	✓

Date	Time	Name	Phone Number	Subject	Follow-up Required	Initials	✓

Date	Time	Name	Phone Number	Subject	Follow-up Required	Initials	✓

Date	Time	Name	Phone Number	Subject	Follow-up Required	Initials	✓

Date	Time	Name	Phone Number	Subject	Follow-up Required	Initials	✓

Date	Time	Name	Phone Number	Subject	Follow-up Required	Initials	✓

Date	Time	Name	Phone Number	Subject	Follow-up Required	Initials	✓

Date	Time	Name	Phone Number	Subject	Follow-up Required	Initials	✓

Date	Time	Name	Phone Number	Subject	Follow-up Required	Initials	✓

Date	Time	Name	Phone Number	Subject	Follow-up Required	Initials	✓

Date	Time	Name	Phone Number	Subject	Follow-up Required	Initials	✓

Date	Time	Name	Phone Number	Subject	Follow-up Required	Initials	✓

Date	Time	Name	Phone Number	Subject	Follow-up Required	Initials	✓

Date	Time	Name	Phone Number	Subject	Follow-up Required	Initials	✓

Date	Time	Name	Phone Number	Subject	Follow-up Required	Initials	✓

Date	Time	Name	Phone Number	Subject	Follow-up Required	Initials	✓

Date	Time	Name	Phone Number	Subject	Follow-up Required	Initials	✓

Date	Time	Name	Phone Number	Subject	Follow-up Required	Initials	✓

Date	Time	Name	Phone Number	Subject	Follow-up Required	Initials	✓

Date	Time	Name	Phone Number	Subject	Follow-up Required	Initials	✓

Date	Time	Name	Phone Number	Subject	Follow-up Required	Initials	✓

Date	Time	Name	Phone Number	Subject	Follow-up Required	Initials	✓

Date	Time	Name	Phone Number	Subject	Follow-up Required	Initials	✓

Date	Time	Name	Phone Number	Subject	Follow-up Required	Initials	✓

Date	Time	Name	Phone Number	Subject	Follow-up Required	Initials	✓

Date	Time	Name	Phone Number	Subject	Follow-up Required	Initials	✓

Date	Time	Name	Phone Number	Subject	Follow-up Required	Initials	✓

Date	Time	Name	Phone Number	Subject	Follow-up Required	Initials	✓

Date	Time	Name	Phone Number	Subject	Follow-up Required	Initials	✓

Date	Time	Name	Phone Number	Subject	Follow-up Required	Initials	✓

Date	Time	Name	Phone Number	Subject	Follow-up Required	Initials	✓

Date	Time	Name	Phone Number	Subject	Follow-up Required	Initials	✓

Date	Time	Name	Phone Number	Subject	Follow-up Required	Initials	✓

Date	Time	Name	Phone Number	Subject	Follow-up Required	Initials	✓

Date	Time	Name	Phone Number	Subject	Follow-up Required	Initials	✓

Date	Time	Name	Phone Number	Subject	Follow-up Required	Initials	✓

Date	Time	Name	Phone Number	Subject	Follow-up Required	Initials	✓

Date	Time	Name	Phone Number	Subject	Follow-up Required	Initials	✓

Date	Time	Name	Phone Number	Subject	Follow-up Required	Initials	✓

Date	Time	Name	Phone Number	Subject	Follow-up Required	Initials	✓

Date	Time	Name	Phone Number	Subject	Follow-up Required	Initials	✓

Date	Time	Name	Phone Number	Subject	Follow-up Required	Initials	✓

Date	Time	Name	Phone Number	Subject	Follow-up Required	Initials	✓

Date	Time	Name	Phone Number	Subject	Follow-up Required	Initials	✓

Date	Time	Name	Phone Number	Subject	Follow-up Required	Initials	✓

Date	Time	Name	Phone Number	Subject	Follow-up Required	Initials	✓

Date	Time	Name	Phone Number	Subject	Follow-up Required	Initials	✓

Date	Time	Name	Phone Number	Subject	Follow-up Required	Initials	✓

Date	Time	Name	Phone Number	Subject	Follow-up Required	Initials	✓

Date	Time	Name	Phone Number	Subject	Follow-up Required	Initials	✓

Date	Time	Name	Phone Number	Subject	Follow-up Required	Initials	✓

Date	Time	Name	Phone Number	Subject	Follow-up Required	Initials	✓

Date	Time	Name	Phone Number	Subject	Follow-up Required	Initials	✓

Date	Time	Name	Phone Number	Subject	Follow-up Required	Initials	✓

Date	Time	Name	Phone Number	Subject	Follow-up Required	Initials	✓

Date	Time	Name	Phone Number	Subject	Follow-up Required	Initials	✓

Date	Time	Name	Phone Number	Subject	Follow-up Required	Initials	✓

Date	Time	Name	Phone Number	Subject	Follow-up Required	Initials	✓

Date	Time	Name	Phone Number	Subject	Follow-up Required	Initials	✓

Date	Time	Name	Phone Number	Subject	Follow-up Required	Initials	✓

Date	Time	Name	Phone Number	Subject	Follow-up Required	Initials	✓

Date	Time	Name	Phone Number	Subject	Follow-up Required	Initials	✓

Date	Time	Name	Phone Number	Subject	Follow-up Required	Initials	✓

Date	Time	Name	Phone Number	Subject	Follow-up Required	Initials	✓

Date	Time	Name	Phone Number	Subject	Follow-up Required	Initials	✓

Date	Time	Name	Phone Number	Subject	Follow-up Required	Initials	✓

Date	Time	Name	Phone Number	Subject	Follow-up Required	Initials	✓

Date	Time	Name	Phone Number	Subject	Follow-up Required	Initials	✓

Date	Time	Name	Phone Number	Subject	Follow-up Required	Initials	✓

Date	Time	Name	Phone Number	Subject	Follow-up Required	Initials	✓

Date	Time	Name	Phone Number	Subject	Follow-up Required	Initials	✓

Date	Time	Name	Phone Number	Subject	Follow-up Required	Initials	✓

Date	Time	Name	Phone Number	Subject	Follow-up Required	Initials	✓

Date	Time	Name	Phone Number	Subject	Follow-up Required	Initials	✓

Date	Time	Name	Phone Number	Subject	Follow-up Required	Initials	✓

Date	Time	Name	Phone Number	Subject	Follow-up Required	Initials	✓

Date	Time	Name	Phone Number	Subject	Follow-up Required	Initials	✓

Date	Time	Name	Phone Number	Subject	Follow-up Required	Initials ✓

Date	Time	Name	Phone Number	Subject	Follow-up Required	Initials	✓

Made in the USA
Middletown, DE
30 June 2025